Mindset Alchemy

Transform Your Life Through Resilience, Discipline, and Timeless Wisdom

Rahul Krishnan

Contents

Chapter 1   Introduction   5

Chapter 2   Understanding Mindset   11

Chapter 3   The Science of Motivation   17

Chapter 4   The Art of Setting Goals   25

Chapter 5   Discipline for a Positive Mindset   33

Chapter 6   Japanese Philosophies   41

Chapter 7   Habits and Routines   49

Chapter 8   Overcoming Obstacles   57

Chapter 9   Mindfulness and Well-being   65

Chapter 10   Relationships and Community   73

Chapter 11   Conclusion – Putting It All Together   81

CHAPTER 1

Introduction

The Power of Mindset
Opening the Door to Change

In the journey of life, our mindset serves as the compass that guides us. The power of mindset is not just a motivational phrase but a scientifically backed reality that has profound implications for our lives. This chapter aims to introduce you to the transformative power of mindset and set the stage for the journey you are about to embark on.

Understanding the Mindset Concept

Mindset, simply put, is the lens through which we view the world. It shapes our thoughts, influences our behaviors, and ultimately determines our outcomes. There are two primary types of mindsets: fixed and growth.

- **Fixed Mindset:** Individuals with a fixed mindset believe that their abilities, intelligence, and talents are static traits that cannot be changed. This belief often leads to a fear of failure, avoidance of challenges, and a tendency to give up easily.

- **Growth Mindset:** In contrast, those with a growth mindset believe that abilities and intelligence can be developed through effort, learning, and persistence. This belief fosters a love for challenges, resilience in the face of setbacks, and a greater potential for success.

The Science Behind Mindset

Research by psychologist Carol Dweck has shown that our mindset profoundly impacts our behavior and achievements. Studies reveal that students with a growth mindset perform better academically, athletes with a growth mindset excel in their sports, and professionals with a growth mindset are more successful in their careers.

Neuroscience supports these findings by showing that our brains are malleable. Through a process called neuroplasticity, our brains can form new connections and pathways, allowing us to learn and grow throughout our lives. This scientific basis underscores the power of adopting a growth mindset.

Real-Life Stories of Transformation

Oprah Winfrey

Oprah Winfrey's journey from a troubled childhood marked by poverty and abuse to becoming one of the most influential media moguls in the world exemplifies the power of a growth mindset. Despite numerous obstacles, she continually sought to learn, improve, and rise above her circumstances.

Walt Disney

Walt Disney faced numerous rejections and failures before creating the iconic Disney empire. His perseverance and willingness to learn from every setback illustrate the essence of a growth mindset. He believed in his ability to improve and achieve his dreams, no matter how many times he was told no.

A personal anecdote: I once met a young entrepreneur named Sarah who had faced multiple business failures by the age of 30. Instead of being discouraged, she viewed each failure as a learning experience. With a growth mindset, she eventually started a successful tech company that now thrives in a competitive market. Her story is a testament to the power of resilience and continuous learning.

Practical Implications of Mindset

Adopting a growth mindset can transform various aspects of your life:

- **Personal Development:** Embrace challenges as opportunities for growth, learn from criticism, and persist in the face of setbacks. These practices will enhance your personal development and lead to greater self-improvement.

- **Relationships:** A growth mindset fosters better communication and empathy. By believing in the potential for growth in yourself and others, you can build stronger, more supportive relationships.

- **Career Success:** In the professional realm, a growth mindset leads to greater innovation, resilience, and a willingness to take on new challenges. These traits are highly valued in today's fast-paced work environment.

- **Health and Well-being:** Studies have shown that individuals with a growth mindset are more likely to adopt healthy behaviors and recover better from illnesses. Believing in your ability to change and improve can positively impact your physical and mental health.

How to Cultivate a Growth Mindset

Cultivating a growth mindset involves intentional practice and self-awareness. Here are some steps to help you get started:

1. **Acknowledge and Embrace Imperfection:** Understand that imperfection is part of the human

experience. Instead of striving for perfection, focus on continuous improvement.

2. **View Challenges as Opportunities:** Reframe challenges as opportunities to learn and grow. Embrace the discomfort that comes with stepping out of your comfort zone.

3. **Learn from Criticism:** Instead of taking criticism personally, use it as constructive feedback to improve. Reflect on the feedback and identify areas for growth.

4. **Celebrate Effort, Not Just Results:** Recognize and celebrate the effort you put into your tasks, regardless of the outcome. This reinforces the value of hard work and persistence.

5. **Cultivate Curiosity:** Stay curious and open to new experiences. Ask questions, seek knowledge, and remain open to learning from different sources.

6. **Practice Self Compassion:** Be kind to yourself during setbacks. Understand that failure is a natural part of the learning process and an opportunity for growth.

The Road Ahead

As you embark on this journey of cultivating a growth mindset, remember that change takes time and effort. The subsequent chapters will provide you with the tools, techniques, and philosophies to support your growth. By embracing a growth mindset, you open the door to endless possibilities and set the foundation for a fulfilling and successful life.

This first chapter serves as a beacon, illuminating the path ahead. With a positive mindset, you have the power to transform your life, achieve your goals, and inspire others along the way. Welcome to the journey of growth and self-discovery.

CHAPTER 2

Understanding Mindset

Fixed vs. Growth Mindset

Fixed Mindset

A fixed mindset is characterized by the belief that our abilities, intelligence, and talents are static and unchangeable. People with a fixed mindset often avoid challenges because they fear failure will expose their limitations. They might give up easily when faced with obstacles, seeing effort as fruitless. Criticism is taken personally, as it's seen as a direct reflection of their inherent abilities. This mindset can lead to a plateau in learning and a reluctance to try new things, limiting personal and professional growth.

Growth Mindset

In contrast, a growth mindset is the belief that abilities and intelligence can be developed through dedication, effort, and learning. People with a growth mindset embrace challenges, viewing them as opportunities to grow. They persist through difficulties, understanding that effort is a crucial component of mastery. Criticism is seen as constructive feedback, and the success of others is inspiring rather than threatening. This mindset fosters resilience, continuous improvement, and a love for learning.

The Science Behind Mindset

Research by Carol Dweck, a pioneering psychologist, has shown that our mindset significantly impacts our behavior, learning, and achievement. Her studies reveal that individuals with a growth mindset tend to achieve more than those with a fixed mindset because they worry less about looking smart and put more energy into learning.

Neuroscience supports this with the concept of neuroplasticity, which is the brain's ability to reorganize itself by forming new neural connections throughout life. This means our brains can grow and change in response to our actions and experiences, reinforcing the idea that we are not limited by our initial abilities or intelligence.

Real-Life Stories of Transformation

Michael Jordan

Michael Jordan, often regarded as the greatest basketball player of all time, is a prime example of a growth mindset. Despite being cut from his high school basketball team, he used this setback as motivation to work harder and improve. His relentless pursuit of excellence and ability to learn from failures were key factors in his legendary career.

J.K. Rowling

Before achieving success with the Harry Potter series, J.K. Rowling faced numerous rejections from publishers and personal hardships. Her belief in her ability to improve and her determination to persevere despite these challenges exemplify a growth mindset. Today, she is one of the most successful authors in history.

Thomas Edison

Thomas Edison, known for inventing the light bulb, had a growth mindset that led him to view failure as a stepping stone to success. He famously said, "I have not failed. I've just found 10,000 ways that won't work." His persistence and willingness to learn from each attempt ultimately led to his breakthrough.

A personal anecdote: During my college years, I struggled significantly with public speaking. My first few attempts were filled with anxiety and stumbling words. However, adopting a growth mindset, I viewed each presentation as a practice opportunity. I sought feedback, practiced diligently, and over time, my skills improved tremendously. This journey not only enhanced my public speaking ability but also boosted my confidence in tackling other challenges.

Practical Implications of Mindset

Adopting a growth mindset can transform various aspects of your life:

- **Personal Development:** Embrace challenges, learn from criticism, and persist in the face of setbacks to enhance personal growth.

- **Relationships:** A growth mindset fosters empathy and understanding, leading to stronger, more supportive relationships.

- **Career Success:** In the professional realm, a growth mindset leads to greater innovation, resilience, and a willingness to take on new challenges.

- **Health and Well-being:** Believing in your ability to change can positively impact your physical and mental health, leading to healthier behaviors and better recovery from illnesses.

Cultivating a Growth Mindset

Cultivating a growth mindset involves intentional practice and self-awareness. Here are some steps to help you get started:

1. **Acknowledge and Embrace Imperfection:** Understand that imperfection is part of the human experience. Focus on continuous improvement rather than perfection.

2. **View Challenges as Opportunities:** Reframe challenges as opportunities to learn and grow. Embrace the discomfort that comes with stepping out of your comfort zone.

3. **Learn from Criticism:** Use criticism as constructive feedback to improve. Reflect on the feedback and identify areas for growth.

4. **Celebrate Effort, Not Just Results:** Recognize and celebrate the effort you put into your tasks, regardless of the outcome. This reinforces the value of hard work and persistence.

5. **Cultivate Curiosity:** Stay curious and open to new experiences. Ask questions, seek knowledge, and remain open to learning from different sources.

6. **Practice Self-Compassion:** Be kind to yourself during setbacks. Understand that failure is a natural part of the learning process and an opportunity for growth.

7. **Surround Yourself with Growth-Oriented People:** Engage with individuals who inspire and challenge you. Being around others who also adopt a growth mindset can reinforce your own efforts and provide a supportive environment.

8. **Visualize Your Growth:** Regularly visualize yourself successfully overcoming challenges and achieving your goals. Visualization can reinforce your belief in your ability to grow and improve.

Exercises to Foster a Growth Mindset

- **Reflective Journaling:** Keep a journal to reflect on your experiences, challenges, and how you've grown from them.

- **Set Learning Goals:** Instead of setting performance goals (e.g., getting an A), set learning goals (e.g., mastering a concept). This shifts the focus from outcomes to the process of learning.

- **Seek Feedback:** Actively seek feedback from others and use it to improve. View it as a tool for growth rather than a judgment of your abilities.

- **Embrace New Challenges:** Regularly take on new challenges that push you out of your comfort zone. Each challenge is an opportunity to grow and learn.

The Road Ahead

As you continue reading, remember that cultivating a growth mindset is a journey, not a destination. The subsequent chapters will provide you with the tools, techniques, and philosophies to support your growth. By embracing a growth mindset, you open the door to endless possibilities and set the foundation for a fulfilling and successful life.

This chapter aims to give readers a thorough understanding of mindset and equip them with practical tools to start shifting their mindset.

CHAPTER 3

The Science of Motivation

Intrinsic vs. Extrinsic Motivation

Intrinsic Motivation

Intrinsic motivation comes from within. It is driven by internal rewards, such as personal satisfaction, curiosity, and the joy of learning. When you are intrinsically motivated, you engage in activities because you find them enjoyable or fulfilling, not because of external rewards or pressures. This type of motivation is powerful and sustainable because it is deeply connected to your interests and passions.

For instance, consider someone who loves painting. They spend hours creating art not for fame or money but because the process itself brings them immense joy and satisfaction. This intrinsic motivation keeps them dedicated and persistent, even when faced with challenges.

Extrinsic Motivation

Extrinsic motivation, on the other hand, is driven by external rewards or pressures, such as money, grades, or approval from others. While extrinsic motivation can be effective in the short term, it often lacks the enduring power of intrinsic motivation. Once the external rewards are removed, the motivation to continue the activity may diminish.

An example of extrinsic motivation is a student studying hard to achieve high grades. While the desire for good grades can drive the student to work diligently, this motivation might wane once the exams are over or if the external reward is no longer appealing.

The Balance Between Intrinsic and Extrinsic Motivation

While intrinsic motivation is ideal for long-term engagement and fulfillment, extrinsic motivation also has its place. The key is to find a balance between the two. External rewards can be useful for initiating behaviors and providing structure, but for sustained motivation, it's crucial to tap into intrinsic motivators.

For example, a person might start exercising to lose weight (extrinsic motivation) but continue because they enjoy the increased energy and well-being (intrinsic motivation). By aligning extrinsic rewards with intrinsic values, you can create a more sustainable and fulfilling motivational system.

Building Lasting Motivation

To maintain motivation over the long term, it's essential to understand what drives you and how to harness these drivers effectively. Here are some strategies to build lasting motivation:

1. **Align Activities with Personal Values**

    Identify your core values and align your activities with them. When your actions are in harmony with your values, you're more likely to feel intrinsically motivated. For instance, if you value creativity, finding ways to incorporate creative tasks into your daily routine can boost your motivation.

2. **Set Meaningful Goals**

    Setting meaningful and purposeful goals can significantly enhance your motivation. Instead of vague objectives, set specific, measurable, achievable, relevant, and time-bound (SMART) goals. Meaningful goals give you a clear direction and a sense of purpose, making it easier to stay motivated.

3. **Celebrate Small Wins**

    Recognize and celebrate your progress, no matter how small. Celebrating small wins provides a sense of accomplishment and boosts your motivation to continue. This can be as simple as acknowledging a completed task or rewarding yourself for reaching a milestone.

4. **Create a Supportive Environment**

   Surround yourself with supportive and like-minded individuals who encourage your growth and development. A positive environment can provide the necessary encouragement and accountability to keep you motivated. Engage in communities or groups that share your interests and goals.

5. **Embrace the Journey**

   Focus on the journey rather than just the destination. Enjoying the process of learning and growing can make the experience more rewarding. When you find joy in the journey, you're more likely to stay motivated and committed, even when faced with challenges.

6. **Find Your "Why"**

   Understanding the deeper reason behind your actions can fuel your motivation. Ask yourself why you want to achieve a particular goal and what it means to you. Connecting your actions to a larger purpose or vision can provide a powerful source of motivation.

Practical Exercises to Boost Motivation

1. **Vision Board**

   Create a vision board that visually represents your goals and aspirations. Include images, quotes, and symbols that inspire you. Place it somewhere you can see daily as a reminder of what you're working towards.

2. **Daily Affirmations**

Practice daily affirmations to reinforce positive beliefs and boost your motivation. Affirmations are positive statements that can help you stay focused and committed. For example, "I am capable of achieving my goals" or "I am motivated and driven."

3. **Motivation Journal**

Keep a motivation journal where you document your progress, challenges, and achievements. Reflecting on your journey can help you stay motivated and identify areas for improvement.

4. **Accountability Partner**

Find an accountability partner who shares similar goals. Regularly check in with each other, share progress, and provide mutual support. Having someone to hold you accountable can enhance your motivation and commitment.

5. **Mindfulness Practice**

Incorporate mindfulness practices to stay present and aware of your motivations. Mindfulness helps you recognize your intrinsic motivations and make conscious choices aligned with your goals.

The Role of Habits in Sustaining Motivation

Habits play a crucial role in sustaining motivation. By creating positive habits, you can make consistent progress towards your goals with less effort. Here's how to develop and maintain effective habits:

1. **Start Small**

   Begin with small, manageable changes. Trying to overhaul your routine overnight can be overwhelming. Instead, focus on building one small habit at a time.

2. **Be Consistent**

   Consistency is key to habit formation. Aim to practice your new habit daily until it becomes a natural part of your routine. The more consistent you are, the more ingrained the habit will become.

3. **Track Your Progress**

   Use a habit tracker to monitor your progress. Seeing a visual representation of your efforts can boost your motivation and provide a sense of accomplishment.

4. **Reward Yourself**

   Reward yourself for sticking to your habits. Positive reinforcement can make the habit-forming process more enjoyable and increase your motivation to continue.

5. **Adjust as Needed**

   Be flexible and willing to adjust your habits if they're not working for you. The goal is to create habits that support your motivation and help you achieve your goals.

The Journey of Building Lasting Motivation

Building lasting motivation is a journey that requires self-awareness, intentional effort, and a willingness to grow. By understanding the science of motivation and applying the strategies and exercises outlined in this chapter, you can cultivate a motivational system that drives you towards success and fulfillment.

As you continue reading this book, remember that motivation is not a one-time event but an ongoing process. Embrace the journey, celebrate your progress, and stay committed to your goals. With a motivated mindset, you have the power to achieve great things and create a life that aligns with your values and aspirations.

This chapter provides readers with a comprehensive understanding of motivation, practical strategies to build and sustain it, and exercises to apply the concepts in their daily lives.

CHAPTER 4

The Art of Setting Goals

The Importance of Goal Setting

Setting goals is fundamental to achieving success and personal fulfillment. Goals provide direction, focus, and a sense of purpose. They act as a roadmap, guiding your actions and decisions. Without clear goals, it's easy to drift aimlessly, lacking motivation and clarity. This chapter will delve into the art of setting effective goals, ensuring they are aligned with your values and aspirations.

SMART Goals

One of the most effective frameworks for setting goals is the SMART criteria. SMART stands for Specific, Measurable, Achievable, Relevant, and Time-bound. Let's break down each component:

- **Specific**

  Goals should be clear and specific, answering the questions of what, why, and how. A specific goal might be, "I want to run a marathon to improve my fitness and achieve a personal milestone."

- **Measurable**

Goals need measurable criteria to track progress. This could be distance, time, or another quantifiable element. For example, "I will train five times a week and gradually increase my running distance."

- **Achievable**

Goals should be realistic and attainable. Setting overly ambitious goals can lead to frustration and demotivation. Ensure your goal is challenging yet achievable given your current resources and constraints.

- **Relevant**

Goals must align with your broader objectives and values. Ask yourself why this goal is important and how it fits into your larger life plan. For instance, "Running a marathon aligns with my values of health and self-improvement."

- **Time-bound**

Every goal needs a deadline to create urgency and focus. A time-bound goal might be, "I will complete the marathon by the end of this year."

The Power of Visualization

Visualization is a powerful tool in goal setting. By vividly imagining the achievement of your goals, you can boost motivation and increase the likelihood of success. Visualization helps to reinforce your commitment and keeps you focused on your desired outcome.

- **Daily Visualization Practice**

  Spend a few minutes each day visualizing the successful achievement of your goals. Picture yourself crossing the finish line, feeling the sense of accomplishment and joy.

- **Vision Board**

  Create a vision board with images and words that represent your goals. Place it somewhere visible to keep your goals top of mind and inspire daily action.

Long-Term Vision and Short-Term Milestones

Balancing long-term vision with short-term milestones is crucial for sustained progress. Long-term goals provide direction, while short-term milestones offer immediate targets to keep you motivated.

- **Long-Term Vision**

  Define your ultimate goals and where you see yourself in the future. These are your overarching aspirations, such as "I want to become a successful entrepreneur."

- **Short-Term Milestones**

  Break down your long-term goals into smaller, manageable steps. For example, if your long-term goal is to start a business, your short-term milestones might include writing a business plan, securing funding, and launching a product.

Practical Tips for Effective Goal Setting

1. **Write Down Your Goals**

   Documenting your goals makes them tangible and reinforces your commitment. Use a journal or digital tool to track your goals and progress.

2. **Create an Action Plan**

   Outline the specific steps you need to take to achieve your goals. An action plan helps to break down the process into manageable tasks and provides a clear roadmap.

3. **Set Priorities**

   Not all goals are created equal. Prioritize your goals based on their importance and urgency. Focus on high-priority goals that have the most significant impact on your life.

4. **Stay Flexible**

   Life is unpredictable, and circumstances may change. Be willing to adjust your goals and action plans as needed. Flexibility allows you to stay on track even when faced with obstacles.

5. **Review and Reflect**

   Regularly review your goals and reflect on your progress. Assess what's working, what's not, and make necessary adjustments. Reflection helps to maintain motivation and ensures you're moving in the right direction.

The Role of Accountability

Accountability is a powerful motivator in achieving goals. Sharing your goals with others and seeking their support can provide encouragement and keep you on track.

- **Accountability Partners**

  Find a friend, mentor, or coach to share your goals with and regularly check in on your progress. An accountability partner can offer support, advice, and motivation.

- **Public Commitment**

  Publicly committing to your goals, such as announcing them on social media or to a group, increases accountability. The fear of public failure can motivate you to stay committed.

Overcoming Obstacles and Staying Committed

Achieving goals is rarely a smooth journey. Obstacles and setbacks are part of the process. Here's how to stay committed:

1. **Anticipate Challenges**

    Identify potential obstacles and plan for how you'll overcome them. Having a plan in place helps to reduce anxiety and keeps you prepared.

2. **Stay Positive**

    Maintain a positive mindset, even in the face of setbacks. Use positive affirmations and visualization to reinforce your commitment and keep your spirits high.

3. **Learn from Setbacks**

    View setbacks as learning opportunities. Reflect on what went wrong, what you can learn from the experience, and how you can improve.

4. **Stay Flexible**

    Be willing to adjust your goals and plans as needed. Flexibility allows you to adapt to changing circumstances without losing sight of your ultimate objectives.

5. **Celebrate Progress**

Recognize and celebrate your progress, no matter how small. Celebrating achievements reinforces positive behavior and keeps you motivated.

Conclusion: The Journey of Goal Setting

Setting and achieving goals is a dynamic and ongoing process. It requires clarity, commitment, and flexibility. By applying the principles and strategies outlined in this chapter, you can set effective goals that inspire and motivate you. Remember, the journey is just as important as the destination. Embrace the process, learn from each step, and enjoy the growth and transformation that come with pursuing your goals.

This chapter provides readers with a comprehensive understanding of effective goal setting, practical strategies, and actionable advice.

CHAPTER 5

Discipline for a Positive Mindset

The Role of Discipline

Discipline is the bridge between goals and accomplishment. It is the ability to stay focused and committed to your goals, even when faced with challenges and distractions. Discipline plays a crucial role in maintaining a positive mindset and achieving long-term success. This chapter will explore the importance of discipline, how to develop it, and its impact on your mindset.

Why Discipline Matters

Discipline is essential for several reasons:

1. **Consistency**

   Discipline ensures that you consistently take action towards your goals, even when motivation wanes. Consistent effort is key to progress and success.

2. **Self-Control**

   Discipline helps you exercise self-control, making it easier to resist temptations and stay focused on what truly matters.

3. **Resilience**

   With discipline, you develop the resilience to overcome setbacks and persevere through difficulties.

4. **Confidence**

   Achieving small, disciplined actions boosts your confidence and belief in your ability to achieve larger goals.

Building Self-Discipline

Developing self-discipline requires intentional practice and commitment. Here are some practical steps to build and strengthen your self-discipline:

1. **Set Clear Goals**

   Define your goals clearly and specifically. Knowing what you want to achieve provides direction and motivation. Break down larger goals into smaller, manageable tasks to avoid feeling overwhelmed.

2. **Create a Routine**

   Establish a daily routine that includes time for work, rest, and personal growth. Routines create structure and help automate disciplined behavior. Stick to your routine consistently to build strong habits.

3. **Eliminate Distractions**

Identify and eliminate distractions that hinder your progress. This might involve setting boundaries with technology, creating a dedicated workspace, or limiting interactions with people who negatively impact your focus.

4. **Practice Delayed Gratification**

Delayed gratification is the ability to resist immediate rewards in favor of long-term benefits. Train yourself to prioritize long-term goals over short-term pleasures. For example, choose to study or work on a project instead of watching TV or scrolling through social media.

5. **Stay Accountable**

Find an accountability partner or join a group where you can share your goals and progress. Accountability provides external motivation and support, making it easier to stay disciplined.

6. **Use Positive Reinforcement**

Reward yourself for staying disciplined and achieving milestones. Positive reinforcement strengthens the behavior and makes it more likely to be repeated.

7. **Visualize Success**

   Regularly visualize the successful achievement of your goals. Visualization reinforces your commitment and helps maintain focus.

8. **Develop Self-Compassion**

   Be kind to yourself when you encounter setbacks. Understand that discipline is a skill that takes time to develop. Learn from your mistakes and continue moving forward.

The Impact of Discipline on Mindset

Discipline and mindset are closely intertwined. Here's how discipline can positively impact your mindset:

1. **Boosts Confidence**

   Consistently following through on your commitments builds self-trust and confidence. Each small victory reinforces your belief in your ability to achieve larger goals.

2. **Reduces Stress**

   Discipline helps you manage your time and responsibilities more effectively, reducing stress and anxiety. Knowing you have a plan and the ability to follow through alleviates the pressure of looming deadlines.

3. **Fosters a Growth Mindset**

   Practicing discipline involves embracing challenges and learning from failures, both of which are key components of a growth mindset. Discipline helps you see obstacles as opportunities for growth.

4. **Enhances Focus**

   Discipline trains your mind to stay focused on the task at hand, improving your concentration and productivity. This focused mindset allows you to make steady progress towards your goals.

5. **Promotes Positivity**

   The satisfaction of achieving goals through disciplined effort fosters a positive outlook. Success breeds success, and each accomplishment encourages you to aim higher.

Practical Exercises to Develop Discipline

1. **Morning Routine**

   Start your day with a structured morning routine that sets a positive tone for the rest of the day. Include activities such as exercise, meditation, and goal-setting.

2. **Time Blocking**

   Use time blocking to allocate specific time slots for different tasks and activities. This method helps you stay organized and ensures that you dedicate time to your most important priorities.

3. **Daily Reflection**

Spend a few minutes each day reflecting on your progress and identifying areas for improvement. This practice promotes self-awareness and helps you stay accountable to your goals.

4. **Habit Stacking**

Build new habits by attaching them to existing ones. For example, if you want to develop a habit of reading daily, do it right after your morning coffee.

5. **Challenge Yourself**

Regularly set small challenges that push you out of your comfort zone. Each challenge strengthens your discipline and resilience.

Overcoming Common Challenges

Building discipline is not without its challenges. Here are some common obstacles and strategies to overcome them:

1. **Procrastination**

Procrastination is a major barrier to discipline. Combat it by breaking tasks into smaller steps, setting deadlines, and using techniques like the Pomodoro Technique to maintain focus.

2. **Lack of Motivation**

Discipline often requires action even when motivation is low. Remind yourself of your "why" and the long-term benefits of staying disciplined. Use visual reminders and affirmations to reinforce your commitment.

3. **Negative Self-Talk**

Negative self-talk can undermine your discipline. Replace self-doubt with positive affirmations and focus on your progress rather than perceived shortcomings. Be your own cheerleader and acknowledge your efforts.

4. **Burnout**

Pushing yourself too hard can lead to burnout. Ensure you balance work and rest, and prioritize self-care to maintain your energy and motivation. Listen to your body and mind, and take breaks when needed.

The Journey of Discipline

Developing discipline is an ongoing journey that requires patience, practice, and perseverance. It's a skill that can be cultivated with consistent effort and a positive mindset. As you continue to build discipline, you'll find that it becomes a natural part of your routine, driving you towards your goals and enhancing your overall well-being.

In the chapters that follow, you'll learn more about integrating discipline with other powerful philosophies and practices to create a holistic approach to personal growth and success.

CHAPTER 6

Japanese Philosophies

Introduction

Japan is renowned for its unique cultural philosophies that offer profound insights into living a meaningful and fulfilling life. These philosophies emphasize balance, mindfulness, continuous improvement, and finding beauty in imperfection. In this chapter, we'll explore several Japanese philosophies that can transform your mindset and approach to life.

Ikigai: Finding Your Reason for Being

Understanding Ikigai

Ikigai (生き甲斐) is a Japanese concept that translates to "a reason for being." It represents the intersection of what you love, what you are good at, what the world needs, and what you can be paid for. Finding your Ikigai involves discovering the activities that bring you joy and fulfillment, while also contributing to the greater good and providing financial sustainability.

Applying Ikigai

1. Self-Reflection

Spend time reflecting on your passions, skills, and values. What activities make you lose track of time? What are you naturally good at?

2. Identify Needs

Consider the needs of the world around you. How can your passions and skills address these needs?

3. Integration

Look for ways to integrate your passions, skills, and societal needs into your career or personal life. This might involve pursuing new opportunities or adjusting your current path to better align with your Ikigai.

Example: A teacher who loves educating, is skilled at engaging students, addresses the need for quality education, and receives a fulfilling salary is living their Ikigai.

Kaizen: Continuous Improvement

Understanding Kaizen

Kaizen (改善) means "continuous improvement." It is a philosophy that encourages small, incremental changes to improve efficiency and quality. Originally applied in business and manufacturing, Kaizen can be applied to personal development, encouraging a mindset of constant growth and improvement.

Applying Kaizen

1. **Set Small Goals**

   Break down larger goals into smaller, manageable steps. Focus on making consistent, incremental improvements.

2. **Embrace Feedback**

   Seek feedback and use it constructively to make continuous improvements.

3. **Reflect and Adjust**

   Regularly reflect on your progress and make adjustments as needed. Celebrate small wins and use them as motivation to keep improving.

Example: An artist who practices Kaizen might focus on improving a specific technique daily, leading to significant progress over time.

Wabi-Sabi: Embracing Imperfection

Understanding Wabi-Sabi

Wabi-Sabi (侘寂) is a Japanese aesthetic that finds beauty in imperfection and impermanence. It encourages us to appreciate the natural cycle of growth and decay, and to accept the flaws and imperfections in ourselves and the world around us.

Applying Wabi-Sabi

1. **Embrace Imperfection**

   Accept that imperfection is a natural part of life. Find beauty in the unique flaws and characteristics that make things special.

2. **Practice Mindfulness**

   Cultivate mindfulness to appreciate the present moment and the transient nature of life.

3. **Simplify**

   Simplify your life by focusing on what truly matters and letting go of unnecessary clutter and perfectionism.

Example: A potter who embraces Wabi-Sabi might cherish the cracks and unevenness in their pottery as unique features that add character and beauty.

Shoshin: Beginner's Mind

Understanding Shoshin

Shoshin (初心) means "beginner's mind." It refers to having an attitude of openness, eagerness, and lack of preconceptions, even when studying at an advanced level. This mindset allows for continuous learning and growth.

Applying Shoshin

1. **Stay Curious**

   Approach every situation with curiosity and a willingness to learn. Ask questions and seek new perspectives.

2. **Let Go of Preconceptions**

   Release any preconceived notions or judgments. Be open to new ideas and experiences.

3. **Embrace Humility**

   Recognize that there is always more to learn. Stay humble and open to growth, regardless of your expertise.

Example: A seasoned software developer who adopts Shoshin might regularly explore new programming languages and techniques with the same enthusiasm as a novice.

Kintsugi: The Art of Golden Repair

Understanding Kintsugi

Kintsugi (金継ぎ) is the art of repairing broken pottery with gold, highlighting the cracks rather than hiding them. It symbolizes the idea that beauty can be found in brokenness and that our experiences, including our scars, contribute to our unique beauty and strength.

Applying Kintsugi

1. **Embrace Your Scars**

   View your past experiences, including failures and hardships, as valuable parts of your journey. They contribute to who you are today.

2. **Heal with Care**

   Approach healing and personal growth with care and intention. Use your experiences to become stronger and more resilient.

3. **Celebrate Growth**

   Celebrate the progress you've made and the person you've become through overcoming challenges.

Example: Someone who has faced significant personal challenges might use Kintsugi as a metaphor for embracing their journey and finding strength in their resilience.

Practical Exercises to Integrate Japanese Philosophies

1. **Ikigai Diagram**

   Create an Ikigai diagram to explore the intersection of your passions, skills, societal needs, and potential for financial sustainability. Reflect on how you can align your life with your Ikigai.

2. **Kaizen Journal**

   Keep a journal to track small, daily improvements. Reflect on your progress and celebrate your achievements, no matter how small.

3. **Wabi-Sabi Meditation**

   Practice mindfulness meditation to appreciate the present moment and the beauty of imperfection. Spend time in nature to connect with the natural cycle of growth and decay.

4. **Shoshin Practice**

   Approach a familiar task or subject with a beginner's mind. Seek out new information, ask questions, and remain open to new ways of thinking.

5. **Kintsugi Reflection**

   Reflect on your past experiences and identify how they have contributed to your growth and resilience. Consider creating a piece of art that symbolizes your journey and the beauty in your imperfections.

Conclusion: Embracing Japanese Philosophies

Integrating these Japanese philosophies into your life can profoundly impact your mindset and overall well-being. They offer timeless wisdom that encourages continuous growth, acceptance of imperfection, and finding meaning and beauty in every aspect of life. As you embrace these philosophies, you'll find yourself more grounded, resilient, and connected to your true self.

CHAPTER 7

Habits and Routines

The Power of Habits

Habits are the building blocks of our daily lives. They shape our actions, influence our decisions, and ultimately determine our success. A habit is a behavior that has been repeated so often that it becomes automatic. Understanding the power of habits and learning how to cultivate positive ones is crucial for personal growth and achieving your goals.

Why Habits Matter

1. **Consistency**

    Habits allow for consistent action without the need for constant decision-making.

2. **Efficiency**

    They reduce mental effort, freeing up cognitive resources for more complex tasks.

3. **Momentum**

   Positive habits create a momentum that drives continuous progress and growth.

4. **Identity**

   Habits reinforce our identity and self-perception, influencing how we see ourselves and how others see us.

Understanding the Habit Loop

The habit loop, as described by Charles Duhigg in "The Power of Habit," consists of three components: cue, routine, and reward.

1. **Cue**

   The trigger that initiates the habit. It can be a time of day, an emotion, a location, or an action.

2. **Routine**

   The behavior or action that follows the cue.

3. **Reward**

   The positive reinforcement that makes the behavior worth repeating.

By understanding and manipulating these components, you can create new habits or change existing ones.

Example:

- **Cue**

  Waking up in the morning.

- **Routine**

  Drinking a glass of water.

- **Reward**

  Feeling refreshed and hydrated.

Creating Positive Habits

Building new, positive habits involves intentional practice and a structured approach. Here's how to create habits that support your goals:

1. **Identify Your Goals**

    Clearly define the goals you want to achieve. Your habits should align with these goals, making them easier to attain.

2. **Start Small**

    Begin with small, manageable changes. Trying to make drastic changes overnight can be overwhelming and unsustainable. Focus on building one small habit at a time.

3. **Use Triggers**

    Identify and use cues that will trigger your desired habit. This could be a specific time, place, or action. Consistency with triggers helps reinforce the habit.

4. **Implement Routine**

   Consistently perform the routine whenever the cue occurs. Repetition is key to ingraining the habit.

5. **Reward Yourself**

   Ensure there is a reward at the end of the routine. This positive reinforcement makes the habit more appealing and increases the likelihood of repetition.

6. **Track Your Progress**

   Keep a habit tracker or journal to monitor your progress. Seeing your consistency can boost motivation and provide a sense of accomplishment.

Breaking Negative Habits

Changing negative habits requires a different approach. Here are some strategies to help you break unwanted habits:

1. **Identify Triggers**

   Recognize the cues that trigger your negative habit. Understanding the triggers is the first step to disrupting the habit loop.

2. **Substitute with Positive Habits**

   Replace the negative habit with a positive one. For example, if you tend to snack on unhealthy foods when stressed, replace it with a healthy alternative or a different stress-relief activity like exercise.

3. **Change Your Environment**

   Modify your environment to reduce exposure to triggers. For instance, if you're trying to quit smoking, avoid places where you typically smoke.

4. **Seek Support**

   Share your goals with friends, family, or a support group. Having others hold you accountable can provide encouragement and motivation.

5. **Practice Self-Compassion**

   Be kind to yourself during the process. Breaking habits is challenging, and setbacks are normal. Learn from them and continue moving forward.

Creating Positive Routines

Routines provide structure and stability, helping you stay focused and productive. Here's how to design routines that support your goals:

1. **Morning Routine**

   A positive morning routine sets the tone for the rest of the day. Include activities that energize and motivate you, such as exercise, meditation, reading, or planning your day.

2. **Work Routine**

    Establish a structured work routine to enhance productivity. This could involve setting specific work hours, taking regular breaks, and prioritizing tasks using techniques like the Pomodoro Technique.

3. **Evening Routine**

    Wind down with an evening routine that promotes relaxation and prepares you for restful sleep. This might include activities like reading, journaling, or practicing gratitude.

4. **Self-Care Routine**

    Incorporate self-care activities into your daily routine to maintain your physical, mental, and emotional well-being. This could involve exercise, healthy eating, and mindfulness practices.

Practical Exercises to Build Habits and Routines

1. **Habit Tracker**

    Use a habit tracker to monitor your daily habits. This visual tool helps you stay accountable and motivated by seeing your progress.

2. **30-Day Challenge**

    Commit to a 30-day challenge to build a new habit. Focusing on one habit for a month increases the likelihood of it becoming ingrained.

3. **Daily Reflection**

   Spend a few minutes each day reflecting on your habits and routines. Identify what's working, what's not, and make adjustments as needed.

4. **Accountability Partner**

   Find an accountability partner to share your habit-building journey with. Regular check-ins and mutual support can enhance your commitment and success.

5. **Mindfulness Practice**

   Incorporate mindfulness practices to stay present and aware of your habits. Mindfulness helps you recognize triggers and make conscious choices.

The Long-Term Impact of Habits and Routines

Developing positive habits and routines has a profound impact on your life. They create a foundation for sustained growth, productivity, and well-being. Over time, these small, consistent actions accumulate, leading to significant progress and transformation.

As you continue to build and refine your habits and routines, you'll find yourself becoming more disciplined, focused, and resilient. The journey of personal growth is ongoing, and habits and routines are essential tools to support you along the way.

In the following chapters, you'll learn more about overcoming obstacles, maintaining mindfulness, and building supportive relationships to further enhance your growth and success.

CHAPTER 8

Overcoming Obstacles

Introduction: The Nature of Obstacles

Obstacles are an inevitable part of life. They come in many forms—personal, professional, physical, emotional—and can often seem insurmountable. However, the way we perceive and respond to these obstacles determines our ability to overcome them and grow. This chapter will explore strategies for overcoming obstacles, building resilience, and using challenges as opportunities for growth.

Embracing a Positive Perspective

Reframing Challenges

One of the most powerful tools in overcoming obstacles is the ability to reframe challenges. Instead of seeing obstacles as barriers, view them as opportunities for learning and growth. This shift in perspective can transform your approach to difficulties and empower you to tackle them head-on.

Growth Mindset

As discussed in previous chapters, adopting a growth mindset is crucial. Believing that abilities can be developed and that challenges are opportunities for improvement fosters resilience and persistence.

Example: Consider Thomas Edison's approach to invention. He viewed each failure as a step closer to success, famously stating, "I have not failed. I've just found 10,000 ways that won't work."

Building Resilience

What is Resilience?

Resilience is the ability to bounce back from adversity, trauma, or significant stress. It involves maintaining flexibility and balance in your life as you deal with stressful circumstances and traumatic events. Resilient people are able to use their experiences to grow and improve their lives.

Strategies to Build Resilience

1. **Develop Strong Connections**

   Cultivate relationships with supportive people. Having a strong social network can provide emotional support, guidance, and encouragement during tough times.

2. **Foster a Positive Self-Image**

Believe in your abilities and maintain a positive view of yourself. Confidence in your strengths helps you tackle challenges more effectively.

3. **Accept Change**

Embrace change as a natural part of life. Accepting what you cannot change allows you to focus on what you can control and adapt accordingly.

4. **Set Realistic Goals**

Break down larger goals into smaller, achievable steps. This approach makes it easier to stay motivated and focused on progress.

5. **Take Decisive Actions**

Act on adverse situations as much as you can. Taking decisive action, rather than detaching from problems and wishing they would go away, helps you face and overcome challenges.

6. **Practice Self-Care**

Prioritize your physical, mental, and emotional well-being. Regular exercise, healthy eating, adequate sleep, and mindfulness practices can enhance your resilience.

7. **Find Purpose**

Engage in activities that provide meaning and purpose. Whether through work, hobbies, or helping others, finding purpose can bolster your resilience.

Practical Techniques for Overcoming Obstacles

1. **Problem-Solving Skills**

   Enhance your problem-solving abilities by breaking down challenges into smaller, manageable parts. Identify potential solutions, weigh their pros and cons, and take actionable steps.

2. **Mindfulness and Stress Management**

   Practice mindfulness to stay present and reduce stress. Techniques such as deep breathing, meditation, and yoga can help manage anxiety and improve focus.

3. **Cognitive Restructuring**

   Challenge negative thought patterns and replace them with positive, constructive ones. Cognitive restructuring helps you maintain a balanced and realistic view of challenges.

4. **Emotional Regulation**

   Learn to manage and regulate your emotions. Techniques such as journaling, talking to a trusted friend, or seeking professional help can provide outlets for processing emotions.

5. **Gratitude Practice**

   Cultivate gratitude by regularly reflecting on the positive aspects of your life. Keeping a gratitude journal can help shift your focus from obstacles to opportunities.

Learning from Failures

Viewing Failure as Feedback

Failure is not the opposite of success; it is a part of the journey. Viewing failure as feedback allows you to learn from your mistakes and make necessary adjustments. Each failure provides valuable insights and lessons that contribute to your growth.

Perseverance and Persistence

Persistence is key to overcoming obstacles. Keep pushing forward, even when faced with setbacks. Remember, many successful people have encountered numerous failures before achieving their goals. Their persistence and determination are what ultimately led them to success.

Example: J.K. Rowling faced numerous rejections before finding a publisher for the Harry Potter series. Her perseverance and belief in her story eventually led to worldwide success.

Seeking Support

The Importance of Asking for Help

Seeking support is not a sign of weakness; it is a recognition of the collective strength we gain from others. Reach out to friends, family, mentors, or professional counselors when you need help. Building a support system can provide new perspectives, advice, and encouragement.

Joining Support Groups

Participate in support groups or communities with similar experiences or goals. Sharing your journey with others who understand your challenges can provide comfort and motivation.

Case Studies: Overcoming Obstacles

Real-Life Examples

1. **Helen Keller:**

    Despite being blind and deaf, Helen Keller became an influential author, political activist, and lecturer. Her story is a testament to the power of resilience, determination, and the support of a dedicated mentor, Anne Sullivan.

2. **Elon Musk:**

    Elon Musk, the CEO of SpaceX and Tesla, faced numerous obstacles, including failed rocket launches and near bankruptcy. Despite these setbacks, Musk's determination and vision led him to revolutionize the space and automotive industries. His ability to persevere through immense challenges showcases extraordinary resilience and innovative thinking.

3. **Nick Vujicic:**

    Born without limbs, Nick Vujicic faced immense physical and emotional challenges. However, he has become a motivational speaker and author, inspiring millions worldwide with his message of hope and resilience.

Conclusion: The Strength in Overcoming Obstacles

Overcoming obstacles is a vital part of personal growth and development. By embracing challenges, building resilience, and

By embracing challenges, building resilience, and learning from failures, you can transform obstacles into opportunities for growth. Remember, the journey of overcoming obstacles is ongoing. With each challenge, you become stronger, more resilient, and better equipped to handle future adversities.

CHAPTER 9

Mindfulness and Well-being

Introduction: The Essence of Mindfulness

Mindfulness is the practice of being fully present and engaged in the current moment, without judgment. It involves awareness of your thoughts, feelings, sensations, and surroundings. Incorporating mindfulness into your daily life can significantly enhance your well-being, reduce stress, and improve mental clarity. This chapter will explore the principles of mindfulness, its benefits, and practical techniques to cultivate mindfulness and well-being.

The Principles of Mindfulness

Being Present

Mindfulness emphasizes living in the present moment rather than dwelling on the past or worrying about the future. By focusing on the here and now, you can experience life more fully and respond to situations with greater clarity and calmness.

Non-Judgmental Awareness

Mindfulness encourages observing your thoughts and feelings without judgment. This means accepting your experiences as they are, without labeling them as good or bad. Non-judgmental awareness fosters self-acceptance and reduces negative self-talk.

Acceptance

Acceptance involves embracing your current reality, even if it includes discomfort or unpleasantness. By accepting your experiences without resistance, you can navigate challenges with greater ease and resilience.

Curiosity and Openness

Approach your experiences with curiosity and openness. This means being willing to explore your thoughts and feelings without preconceived notions or judgments. Curiosity fosters a deeper understanding of yourself and your reactions.

Benefits of Mindfulness

Reduced Stress

Mindfulness has been shown to reduce stress by promoting relaxation and reducing the physiological effects of stress. Practicing mindfulness can help lower cortisol levels, decrease heart rate, and improve overall stress management.

Improved Mental Clarity

Regular mindfulness practice enhances mental clarity and focus. By training your mind to stay present, you can improve your concentration, decision-making, and problem-solving abilities.

Enhanced Emotional Regulation

Mindfulness helps you become more aware of your emotions and how they influence your behavior. This awareness allows you to respond to emotions more skillfully, reducing impulsive reactions and improving emotional regulation.

Increased Well-being

Mindfulness contributes to overall well-being by promoting a sense of peace, contentment, and fulfillment. It can enhance your relationships, increase self-awareness, and improve your quality of life.

Practical Mindfulness Techniques

Mindful Breathing

Mindful breathing is a foundational mindfulness practice. It involves paying attention to your breath, noticing each inhale and exhale. This practice can be done anywhere, anytime, and serves as an anchor to bring you back to the present moment.

Body Scan Meditation

Body scan meditation involves mentally scanning your body from head to toe, noticing any areas of tension or discomfort. This practice promotes relaxation and body awareness, helping you connect with your physical sensations.

Loving-Kindness Meditation

Loving-kindness meditation focuses on cultivating compassion and kindness towards yourself and others. It involves silently repeating phrases such as "May I be happy, may I be healthy, may I be safe," and extending these wishes to others.

Mindful Walking

Mindful walking is the practice of walking slowly and deliberately, paying attention to the sensations in your feet and the movement of your body. This practice can be done in nature or any quiet space, helping you connect with your surroundings.

Gratitude Practice

Cultivating gratitude involves regularly reflecting on the things you are thankful for. Keeping a gratitude journal, where you write down things you appreciate each day, can enhance your sense of well-being and positivity.

Incorporating Mindfulness into Daily Life

1. **Start Small:** Begin with short mindfulness practices, such as a few minutes of mindful breathing each day. Gradually increase the duration as you become more comfortable with the practice.

2. **Create Mindful Rituals:** Incorporate mindfulness into your daily routines. This could include mindful eating, where you savor each bite of your meal, or mindful listening, where you fully engage in conversations without distractions.

3. **Set Reminders:** Use reminders, such as alarms or sticky notes, to prompt you to practice mindfulness throughout the day. These reminders can help you stay present and focused.

4. **Practice Gratitude:** Incorporate gratitude into your daily routine by reflecting on things you are thankful for each morning or evening. This practice can shift your focus from what's lacking to what's abundant in your life.

5. **Engage in Mindful Activities:** Engage in activities that promote mindfulness, such as yoga, tai chi, or gardening. These activities encourage you to be present and fully engaged in the moment.

Mindfulness in Challenging Times

Mindfulness is particularly valuable during challenging times. Here's how to apply mindfulness to navigate difficulties:

1. **Acknowledge Your Feelings**

   Recognize and accept your emotions without judgment. Allow yourself to feel without trying to suppress or change your emotions.

2. **Stay Present**

   Focus on the present moment, rather than getting lost in worries about the future or regrets about the past. Use mindful breathing or grounding techniques to stay anchored in the here and now.

3. **Practice Self-Compassion**

   Be kind to yourself during tough times. Treat yourself with the same compassion you would offer a friend facing similar challenges.

4. **Seek Support**

   Reach out to friends, family, or support groups for emotional support. Sharing your experiences with others can provide comfort and perspective.

5. **Engage in Mindful Activities**

   Engage in activities that bring you peace and joy. This could include spending time in nature, practicing creative hobbies, or engaging in physical exercise.

Conclusion: The Journey of Mindfulness

Mindfulness is a journey of self-discovery and personal growth. By incorporating mindfulness into your daily life, you can enhance your well-being, reduce stress, and cultivate a deeper connection with yourself and the world around you. Remember, mindfulness is not about achieving a perfect state of peace, but about being present and fully engaged in each moment.

In the following chapters, you'll learn more about building supportive relationships, giving back to your community, and integrating the principles and techniques discussed so far into a holistic approach to personal growth and success.

CHAPTER 10

Relationships and Community

Introduction: The Importance of Relationships

Human beings are inherently social creatures. Our relationships and sense of community play a crucial role in our overall well-being, happiness, and personal growth. Building and nurturing positive relationships can provide support, encouragement, and a sense of belonging. This chapter explores the significance of relationships, how to build supportive networks, and the impact of giving back to the community.

Building Supportive Relationships

Understanding Supportive Relationships

Supportive relationships are those in which individuals provide mutual respect, encouragement, and assistance. These relationships can be with family, friends, colleagues, or mentors. They are built on trust, communication, and empathy.

Key Elements of Supportive Relationships

1. **Trust**

   Trust is the foundation of any strong relationship. It involves honesty, reliability, and integrity. Building trust takes time and consistency.

2. **Communication**

   Effective communication is essential for understanding and connection. This includes active listening, expressing yourself clearly, and being open to feedback.

3. **Empathy**

   Empathy is the ability to understand and share the feelings of another. It involves being present, showing compassion, and validating others' experiences.

4. **Respect**

   Respect involves valuing each other's opinions, boundaries, and individuality. It means appreciating differences and treating each other with dignity.

5. **Support**

   Providing support means being there for each other in times of need. This can involve offering a listening ear, practical help, or emotional encouragement.

Building and Maintaining Positive Relationships

1. **Be Authentic**

    Authenticity is key to building genuine relationships. Be yourself and encourage others to do the same. Authenticity fosters trust and deeper connections.

2. **Show Appreciation**

    Regularly express gratitude and appreciation for the people in your life. Acknowledging their contributions and presence strengthens bonds.

3. **Invest Time**

    Spend quality time with your loved ones. Whether it's through regular catch-ups, shared activities, or meaningful conversations, investing time is crucial for nurturing relationships.

4. **Practice Active Listening**

    Listen attentively to others without interrupting or judging. Active listening shows that you value their thoughts and feelings.

5. **Be Supportive**

    Offer support when needed, whether it's emotional, practical, or financial. Being a reliable source of support strengthens trust and loyalty.

6. **Resolve Conflicts**

   Address conflicts openly and constructively. Avoiding or suppressing issues can harm relationships. Approach conflicts with empathy and a willingness to find solutions.

The Role of Community

Understanding Community

A community is a group of individuals who share common values, interests, or goals. Being part of a community provides a sense of belonging, purpose, and support. Communities can be based on location, interests, professions, or shared experiences.

Benefits of Community Involvement

1. **Support and Encouragement**

   Communities provide a support network that can offer help and encouragement during challenging times.

2. **Shared Knowledge and Resources**

   Being part of a community allows you to share knowledge, skills, and resources, enhancing personal and collective growth.

3. **Increased Well-being**

   Community involvement is linked to improved mental and emotional well-being. It fosters a sense of purpose and connection.

4. **Opportunities for Contribution**

   Communities offer opportunities to give back and make a positive impact. Contributing to your community can provide a sense of fulfillment and satisfaction.

Building a Supportive Community

1. **Join Groups or Organizations**

   Participate in groups or organizations that align with your interests or values. This could be clubs, professional associations, or volunteer organizations.

2. **Engage in Community Activities**

   Attend community events, workshops, or social gatherings. Engaging in community activities helps you connect with like-minded individuals.

3. **Contribute Your Skills**

   Offer your skills and expertise to benefit the community. Whether it's through volunteering, mentoring, or sharing knowledge, your contributions can make a difference.

4. **Foster Inclusivity**

   Promote inclusivity and diversity within your community. Embrace different perspectives and create an environment where everyone feels welcome and valued.

5. **Build Strong Relationships**

   Focus on building strong, positive relationships within your community. These relationships can provide mutual support and encouragement.

The Power of Giving Back

Why Giving Back Matters

Giving back to your community or those in need has numerous benefits. It fosters a sense of purpose, enhances well-being, and strengthens social bonds. Acts of kindness and generosity can have a ripple effect, inspiring others to do the same.

Ways to Give Back

1. **Volunteering**

   Offer your time and skills to support causes you care about. Volunteering can range from helping at local shelters to participating in community clean-ups.

2. **Mentoring**

   Share your knowledge and experience by mentoring someone. Mentorship can provide guidance, support, and inspiration to others.

3. **Charitable Donations**

   Contribute financially to organizations or causes that align with your values. Donations can help support important initiatives and provide resources to those in need.

4. **Acts of Kindness**

Perform small acts of kindness in your daily life. This could be helping a neighbor, supporting a friend, or simply offering a smile to a stranger.

5. **Advocacy**

Advocate for causes and issues that matter to you. Use your voice and platform to raise awareness and drive positive change.

Practical Exercises to Strengthen Relationships and Community

1. **Gratitude Letters**

Write letters of gratitude to people who have made a positive impact in your life. Expressing appreciation can strengthen your relationships and spread positivity.

2. **Weekly Check-Ins**

Schedule regular check-ins with friends, family, or community members. These check-ins can be casual conversations or more structured discussions about goals and well-being.

3. **Community Projects**

Participate in or initiate community projects that address local needs or interests. Collaborating on projects can foster a sense of unity and purpose.

4. **Random Acts of Kindness**

   Practice random acts of kindness regularly. These small gestures can brighten someone's day and create a positive ripple effect.

5. **Join a Support Group**

   If you're facing specific challenges, consider joining a support group. Sharing experiences with others who understand can provide comfort and guidance.

Conclusion: The Journey of Relationships and Community

Building and nurturing supportive relationships and engaging with your community are essential components of a fulfilling life. By investing time and effort into these areas, you can create a strong support network, enhance your well-being, and make a positive impact on the world around you.

CHAPTER 11

Conclusion – Putting It All Together

Recap of Key Concepts

Throughout this book, we've explored various principles, techniques, and philosophies aimed at fostering a positive mindset, building resilience, and achieving personal growth. Let's revisit some of the key concepts covered:

1. **Mindset**

   - The difference between a fixed and growth mindset.

   - The importance of adopting a growth mindset to embrace challenges and view failures as opportunities for growth.

2. **Motivation**

   - Understanding intrinsic and extrinsic motivation.

- Strategies to build lasting motivation by aligning activities with personal values and setting meaningful goals.

3. **Goal Setting**

- The SMART criteria for setting effective goals.

- Balancing long-term vision with short-term milestones to ensure continuous progress.

4. **Discipline**

- The role of discipline in achieving a positive mindset.

- Practical steps to build and maintain self-discipline.

5. **Japanese Philosophies**

- Ikigai: Finding your reason for being.

- Kaizen: Continuous improvement.

- Wabi-Sabi: Embracing imperfection.

- Shoshin: Beginner's mind.

- Kintsugi: The art of golden repair.

6. **Habits and Routines**

- The power of habits in shaping our actions and decisions.

- Techniques to build positive habits and routines.

7. **Overcoming Obstacles**

    - Strategies for overcoming challenges and building resilience.

    - Viewing failures as feedback and opportunities for growth.

8. **Mindfulness and Well-being**

    - The principles of mindfulness and its benefits.

    - Practical mindfulness techniques to enhance well-being.

9. **Relationships and Community**

    - Building supportive relationships and the importance of community.

    - The power of giving back and its impact on personal fulfillment.

Integrating the Principles

The journey towards personal growth and a positive mindset is ongoing. Integrating the principles discussed in this book requires intentional practice and a commitment to continuous improvement. Here are some steps to help you integrate these principles into your daily life:

1. **Self-Reflection:**

    - Regularly reflect on your thoughts, actions, and progress. Use journaling or meditation to gain insights and identify areas for growth.

2. **Set Clear Intentions:**

   - Start each day with clear intentions. Outline your goals, priorities, and the mindset you want to cultivate. This sets a positive tone for the day.

3. **Practice Consistency:**

   - Consistency is key to forming new habits and achieving long-term goals. Commit to daily practices that align with the principles discussed, such as mindfulness exercises, goal-setting, and positive routines.

4. **Seek Support:**

   - Surround yourself with supportive people who encourage your growth. Share your journey with friends, family, or a mentor who can provide guidance and accountability.

5. **Embrace Flexibility:**

   - Life is unpredictable, and circumstances may change. Be flexible and willing to adjust your plans and goals as needed. Adaptability is crucial for maintaining progress.

Actionable Steps for Continued Growth

1. **Create a Vision Board:**

   - Visualize your goals and aspirations by creating a vision board. Include images, quotes, and symbols that inspire you. Place it somewhere you can see daily to stay motivated.

2. **Develop a Daily Routine:**

    * Establish a daily routine that includes time for self-care, mindfulness, and goal-oriented activities. A structured routine promotes consistency and discipline.

3. **Set Monthly Goals:**

    * Break down your long-term goals into monthly milestones. Review and adjust your goals regularly to stay on track and celebrate your progress.

4. **Engage in Lifelong Learning:**

    * Commit to continuous learning and personal development. Read books, attend workshops, and seek new experiences that expand your knowledge and skills.

5. **Practice Gratitude:**

    * Cultivate a gratitude practice by reflecting on the positive aspects of your life. Keep a gratitude journal and regularly express appreciation to others.

6. **Give Back:**

    * Find ways to give back to your community or support causes you care about. Volunteering,

mentoring, or performing acts of kindness can provide a sense of purpose and fulfillment.

The Journey Forward

Personal growth and a positive mindset are lifelong journeys. As you continue to apply the principles and techniques discussed in this book, remember that progress is not always linear. There will be ups and downs, but each step forward brings you closer to your goals and a more fulfilling life.

Stay committed to your growth, be kind to yourself, and embrace the process. The journey of self-discovery and improvement is one of the most rewarding endeavors you can undertake. By cultivating a positive mindset, building resilience, and fostering supportive relationships, you have the power to create a life that aligns with your values and aspirations.

Final Words of Encouragement

You have the tools and knowledge to transform your life. Embrace each day with an open mind, a positive attitude, and a willingness to learn and grow. Remember, the power to create a fulfilling and successful life lies within you.

Thank you for embarking on this journey of growth and self-discovery. May you continue to thrive, overcome challenges, and inspire others along the way. Be radiant, and let your positive mindset shine brightly in all that you do.

www.ingramcontent.com/pod-product-compliance
Lightning Source LLC
Chambersburg PA
CBHW031323130726
47988CB00007B/2952